ANSWER SONG

Also by David Trinidad

Pavane

Monday, Monday

Living Doll

November

Hand Over Heart

David Trinidad

ANSWER SONG

LONDON / NEW YORK

First published 1994 by
High Risk Books/Serpent's Tail
4 Blackstock Mews, London, England N4 2BT
and 401 West Broadway, New York, NY 10012

Library of Congress Cataloging-in-Publication Data

Trinidad, David, 1953–
        Answer song / David Trinidad.
                p.   cm.
        ISBN 1-85242-329-3
        I. Title.
        PS3570.R53A83   1994   94-21997
        811'.54—dc20   CIP

Book and cover design by Rex Ray
Typeset in Janson 11/5 and Futura Condensed by *Loose Amalgam*
Printed in Hong Kong by Colorcraft
10 9 8 7 6 5 4 3 2 1

Acknowledgments

I am grateful to the editors of the following magazines and anthologies, in which much of the work in this book has previously appeared:

A New Geography of Poets, *B City*, *BOMB*, **Broadway 2**, *Brooklyn Review*, *City Lights Review*, *Columbia*, *CUZ*, **Discontents**, *Exact Change Yearbook*, *Gas*, *GIRLJOCK*, **High Risk**, *The Illinois Review*, *Instant Classics*, *The James White Review*, **Mondo Barbie**, *New American Writing*, *New Delta Review*, *New Observations*, *OutWeek*, *Pequod*, **Poets For Life**, *Santa Monica Review*, *Shiny*, **Stand Up Poetry**, *St. Mark's Poetry Project Newsletter*, **That Various Field**, **Walk on the Wild Side**, *WHAT!*, and *The World*.

I am also grateful to the following individuals for their friendship and support: Jeffery Conway, Jim Cory, Lynn Crosbie, Elaine Equi, Amy Gerstler, Robyn Selman, and Susan Wheeler.

Special thanks to Pete Ayrton and Amy Scholder.

D.T.

for Ira

Contents

1

Pleasant Street

Your neighbor
waves and waters
her flowerpots

(red geraniums)
as the trees gently
shake off and

litter the side-
walk with their
yellow leaves.

The cat sits at
the open window.
The teacup steams.

The mail comes
early: the world
wants your poems!

The best years
of your last life
glide by like

someone whistling
your favorite song.

Driving Back from New Haven

Tim looks at his watch, reaches into his
pocket, takes out a small plastic container
and swallows an AZT pill with a sip of Sprite.
"Poison," he mutters under his breath. I
glance over at him. We haven't talked about
his health the entire trip. "How does it
make you feel?" I ask. "Like I want to live
until they discover a cure," he snaps. We
travel in silence for a while. I stare out
the window at all the green trees on the
Merritt Parkway. Then he says: "I resent
it. I resent that we were not raised with
an acceptance of death. And here it is,
all around us. And I fucking resent it.
I resent that we do not know how to die."

Locus Solus

for James Schuyler

Six floors up:
sunlight from
23rd St. Tom's
cat (Barbara)
on top of desk
next to orange
& white scarf
(on typewrit-
er). Apples on
tv. Diet Pepsi.
Leaf taped to
mirror. Stacks
of mysteries.
Porter & Park
(your book cov-
ers) on walls.
Flowers (yel-
low & salmon
carnations in
blue bottle,
lilies in tall
vase). Fortune
from tonight's
take-out: *You
will soon be
crossing the
great waters.*

Well I Wonder

Much despair
in his lyrics.
Candle flicker-
ing. Trembling
at the thought
of your touch.

Hockney: Blue Pool

Los Angeles,
California:
a summer afternoon.
One boy sunbathes
on a yellow towel
beside the pool;
another stands
at the end of
the diving board,
gazing downward.
Palm trees sway
in the blue water.
Overhead, a few
clouds float by.
To the right,
sprinklers lightly
spray the green
lawn. The sunbather
slips off his red
and white striped
swimsuit and rolls
over; the other
boy dives into the
pool. The artist
snaps a photograph
of the splash.

Song

"You Don't Own Me"
was a hit that summer. Up in
my room, I played
it till the single was all scratched

while, below, my
brother's friends caught softballs in the
street. They drove me
nuts as the song, all summer long.

My Lover

My lover who is black
My lover who is blond
My lover who is Italian
My lover who is well-hung
My lover who sucks my toes
My lover who has thick lips
My lover who swallows my cum
My lover who licks my armpits
My lover who cums in my mouth
My lover who cums all over me
My lover who cums inside of me
My lover who has a perfect ass
My lover who wears a jockstrap
My lover who wears cowboy boots
My lover who pinches my nipples
My lover who likes Rachmaninoff
My lover who gives me gonorrhea
My lover who leaves his socks on
My lover who will not French kiss
My lover who doesn't know my name
My lover who fucks me standing up
My lover who sleeps on Vera sheets
My lover who is drenched with sweat
My lover who bleeds when I fuck him
My lover who completely undresses me
My lover who refuses to have safe sex

My lover who is my ex-lover's ex-lover
My lover who sucks my tongue when I cum
My lover who fucks me for the first time
My lover who plunges his tongue into my ear
My lover who drapes his legs over my shoulders
My lover who gropes me as I pass through the crowd
My lover who sticks three of his fingers up my ass
My lover who kisses me at midnight on New Year's Eve
My lover who rubs the crotch of his faded blue jeans
My lover who rapes me at knifepoint without lubricant
My lover who reaches into my pants while I play pinball
My lover who sucks me off in the bushes in Lafayette Park
My lover who presses his cock against mine as we slow
    dance
My lover who licks a drop of pre-cum from the tip of
    my dick
My lover who vomits on me in the middle of sex and
    passes out
My lover who pulls me by the cock to a corner of the
    orgy room
My lover who goes down on me in a parked car in the
    pouring rain
My lover who pins my arms above my head and kisses me
    long and hard
My lover who holds a bottle of amyl to his nose just before
    he shoots his load
My lover who plays "Killing Me Softly With His Song"
    over and over as we make love all afternoon

2

Love Poem

At 4:30 a.m., I wake up
from a nightmare, bump
through the dark apartment
to pee, then sit and smoke
a cigarette in the living
room. When I get back
in bed, Ira wakes up
and says: "You're a sweet
man, do you know that?"
I tell him I've been having
bad dreams. I'm lying on
my back; he tells me to roll
on my side. As I do, he presses
against me from behind and
wraps his arm around my chest.
"You're safe now," he whispers
into my neck. "Go back to sleep.
You won't have any more bad dreams."

Last Night

Ira knocked

one of the mums

in the makeshift vase

(a blue glass)

beside the bed

in his sleep

and we woke up

with white petals

in between

the sheets

Sunday Evening

Back from Boston,
Ira and I listen
to a tape of Anne Sexton
reading her poems—
part of my $87.00 binge
at the Grolier Book Shop
in Harvard Square.
Ira likes her "smoky" voice,
which is interrupted
by the kettle's shrill whistle.
I go into the kitchen
and prepare our tea:
Cranberry Cove for Ira,
Mellow Mint for me.
We sip, smoke and listen
to Anne. Toward the end
of the tape, Ira unpacks
the little black bag
of Godiva chocolates
and, one by one, eats
a butterscotch-filled coat
of arms, a light brown starfish
and a gold-foiled cherry cordial.
He chews and smiles.
I regret that I ate all
of mine on the train.
But wait! He offers me
his last one (which he
makes me earn with kisses):
a dark chocolate heart.

Wednesday Morning

After three
or four
hours sleep,
the news
comes on
the clock
radio and
Ira nudges me.

"Snooze,"
I mumble.

"I know it's
the news," he
says, nudging
me again.
"Turn it off."

"*Snooze*,"
I say,
"not *news*."

Then I tell
him my dream:
John and Yoko
were in it

and every
time someone
said "moon,"
everyone else
chanted "moon
moon moon
moon moon
moon moon."

"Sounds like
the secret word
on *Pee-wee's
Playhouse*,"
he says.

"No, it isn't
the same thing."

Then I push
the Snooze button
and we both go
back to sleep.

Dead Flowers

So how did you know I was having bad dreams?

Because you woke up and told me—
just like in that poem.

*That's right. I dreamt I was watering dead violets.
But then you said something . . .*

I said: "Dead flowers are for faggots."

That's right. Why did you say that?

Because when I was a freshman in high school
my art teacher told us to draw some dead flowers
and this guy in the class said:
"Dead flowers are for faggots."

How weird.

I know. But for a long time
I thought it was true because that guy said it:
"Dead flowers are for faggots."

3

Pee Shy

I waited till
the boys' room
was empty, then
stood at one
of the urinals.
It always took
me a long
time, even when
I was alone.
Before I could
do it, someone
came in and
stood next to
me. Anxiously, I
glanced over. It
was Steve, the
good-looking son
of an actor
on a popular
detective series. He
was one grade
ahead of me.
Everyone said he
was stuck-up,
but I'd always
had a crush

on him. As
we stood beside
each other, my
legs began to
shake. I tried
to look straight
at the wall
in front of
me. Without realizing
it, however, I
pressed my whole
body against the
urinal. "Don't worry,"
Steve said disdainfully,
"I'm not looking
at you." He
pulled the handle
above his urinal,
zipped up his
pants. Out of
the corner of
my eye, I
watched him wash
his hands and
check his hair
in the mirror.
Then he left.

I can't remember
anything after that.
How long did

I stand there?
Did I rush
to my locker?
Was I late
for a period
I dreaded—woodshop,
drafting, gym? How
did I hide
my shame, convinced
as I was—
as I'm sure
I was—that
everyone would know
my hideous secret
before I even reached
my next class?

Playing with Dolls

Every weekend morning, I'd sneak downstairs to play
with my sisters' Barbie dolls. They had all
of them: Barbie, Ken, Allan, Midge, Skipper and
Skooter. They even had the little freckled boy,
Ricky ("Skipper's Friend"), and Francie, "Barbie's
'MOD'ern cousin." Quietly, I'd set the dolls

in front of their wardrobe cases, take the dolls'
clothes off miniature plastic hangers, and play
until my father woke up. There were several Barbies—
blonde ponytail, black bubble, brunette flip—all
with the same pointed tits, which (odd for a boy)
didn't interest me as much as the dresses and

accessories. I'd finger each glove and hat and
necklace and high heel, then put them on the dolls.
Then I'd invent elaborate stories. A "creative" boy,
I could entertain myself for hours. I liked to play
secretly like that, though I often got caught. All
my father's tirades ("Boys don't play with Barbies!

It isn't *normal*!") faded as I slipped Barbie's
perfect figure into her stunning ice blue and
sea green satin and tulle formal gown. All
her outfits had names like "Fab Fashion," "Doll's
Dream" and "Golden Evening"; Ken's were called "Play
Ball!," "Tennis Pro," "Campus Hero" and "Fountain Boy,"

which came with two tiny sodas and spoons. Model boy
that he was, Ken hunted, fished, hit home runs. Barbie's
world revolved around garden parties, dances, play
and movie dates. A girl with bracelets and scarves and
sunglasses and fur stoles. . . . "Boys don't play with dolls!"
My parents were arguing in the living room. "All

boys do." As always, my mother defended me. "All
sissies!" snarled my father. "He's a creative boy,"
my mother responded. I stuffed all the dresses and dolls
and shoes back into the black cases that said "Barbie's
Wonderful World" in swirling pink letters and
clasped them shut. My sisters, awake now, wanted to play

with me. "I can't play," I said, "Dad's upset." All
day, he stayed upset. Finally, my mother came upstairs
    and said: "You're a boy,
David. Forget about Barbies. Stop playing with dolls."

(Doll Not Included)

c
e k
n l
e a
c

apinks
carfco
mplete
stheen
semble

ack
l p s
b ump

glamouri
nthespot
lighta
sbarb
iesin
gsofbitt
ersweetlov
eandteenag
eheartachesh
erskintigh
tglitter
knitbl
ackf
orma
lmov
esin
toaf
rilloftu
lleatthche
mwithasinglere
dsatinroseaccent

pu re

*

she
adj
ust

s
t
h
e
s
i
l
v
e
r
y
m
i
c
r
o

phonetoth
eproperheight

lo
ng
bl
ac
kt
ri
co
tg
lov
es

Family Portrait, 1963

My father sits in his dark
armchair, under a store-bought
painting of Paris,
reading *Fortune* magazine.
As a young man
he read Shakespeare and Poe,
dreamed of being an artist
(my mother tells me this).
Now he works somewhere
every day, and at night
barks orders: *Sit up*
straight! Get out
of my sight! Stop
that racket! Goddamnit!
Turn down the TV!

•

My mother sobs
behind her locked bedroom door:
Your father's a tyrant.
Go away. Other nights
she has migraines
and lies in agony
on the living room couch
while my father yells

Get up, you fat slob!
Do some work around here!
I do chores for her, sneak
her cigarettes and chocolate bars
into the house, hide them
in the pots and pans.
When they fight, I lock
myself in the pink bathroom,
play with the soap roses
in the shell-shaped dish,
with her delicate perfume bottles
and her Avon lipsticks—
so many names for red.

●

My brother collects
baseball cards,

                    for my father

builds model airplanes
and race cars,

                    for my father

watches *Gunsmoke*
and *Combat*,

                    for my father

joins Boy Scouts
and Little League,

                    for my father

mows the lawn,
pulls the weeds,
rakes the leaves,

>*for my father*

excels in batting
and tackling
and running,

>*for my father*

and brings home
poor grades on
his report card.

And is punished
by my father.

•

One of my sisters stands
at a miniature bassinet
changing the diaper
on her Hush-a-Bye Baby.
(Someday she'll have four
children of her own, bounced
checks, bruises and black eyes,
a husband she'll try, repeatedly,
to leave.) With a makebelieve
iron, she unwrinkles the doll's
frilly pink party frock.
She's my father's favorite:
the quietest one.

•

My other sister learns
to walk early, is always
breaking things. One night,
when my father barks an order
at the dinner table, she puts her
little hands on her hips
and barks back: *You're
not the boss! I am!*
After a tense silence,
my father's face seems to
crack, and he laughs.
Then we all laugh.

•

At school, I spend
most of the lunch hour
in the library.
I belong to
the Bookworm Club:
the more I read,
the higher my name moves up
the bespectacled paper worm
on the bulletin board.
I'm reading the *Little House*
series and the blue biographies
of famous Americans,
but only the women:
Pocahontas, Martha Washington,
Betsy Ross.

In the afternoon,
I do homework
at the kitchen table
while my mother cooks and cleans.
I ask her questions,
but there's a lot she doesn't know.
She hands me a warm Toll House cookie,
tells me to look for the answer
in the book.

Around 4:30, she sprays
lilac-scented Glade
to cover up the smell
of her cigarettes.

When my father's car
pulls in the driveway,
she franticly sets out
napkins, glasses, handfuls
of silverware.
Make yourself scarce.
I gather my books and papers
together, rush down the hall
to my bedroom, hear
the door slam.

Invasion

Kevin McCarthy knows what is happening.
Unwittingly, he's discovered something odd:
Aliens are posing as human beings.

One by one, all the townspeople are changing.
It happens right after they give you a pod.
Kevin McCarthy knows what is happening.

While you sleep, the pod duplicates your body.
Crackling, your flesh shrivels into a lifeless wad.
Aliens are posing as human beings.

When you wake up, you don't have any feelings.
You look perfectly normal, but you're a fraud.
Kevin McCarthy knows what is happening.

Franticly, he runs through the streets screaming
Run for your life! They're here! They're here!
   Oh my God!
Aliens are posing as human beings!

He knows he can't take speed and drink coffee
forever. Eventually, he'll start to nod.
Kevin McCarthy knows what is happening:
Aliens are posing as human beings.

The Bomb Shelter

The photograph on the front page of the paper showed a supermarket after an attack of mass hysteria: shelves stripped bare as Old Mother Hubbard's. At home, my mother filled our pantry with cans of Campbell's soup and Spam, while my father—who had quit smoking on the very day the Surgeon General announced that cigarettes could be hazardous to health—hired a contractor to install a bomb shelter in our backyard. Our dream of a swimming pool (my brother and sisters and I were always begging our parents to put one in) went up in smoke as, out of nowhere, a crew of potbellied construction workers appeared and started digging in the same spot we'd buried a pet turtle, goldfish, rabbit, and guinea pig. A few months later, my father proudly took us on a tour. We climbed down a ladder and huddled in darkness behind him. Like a strict teacher pointing at a blackboard with a stick, he waved his flashlight at a couple of sleeping bags and boxes of provisions, at a port-a-potty, and at the handle of the air vent we'd all have to take turns rotating in order to breathe. "Will I be able to bring my comic books?" I asked. "No. No toys." In the first place, my family were the last people on earth I wanted to sit with in a tiny subterranean room with a port-a-potty and a five-month supply of Spam and wait however long it took for the radiation to wear off. But without my comic books, I decided it would be better to take my chances above ground. I wondered if they would drop The Bomb while I was at school. In Mrs. Bialosky's class, we'd started having drills. Suddenly, in the middle of a lesson, she'd call out "Drop," and we'd all crouch underneath our desks with our hands cupped over our heads. My parents informed us that we were not to tell any of our friends about the bomb shelter. It was a secret. If there were a war, they explained, our neighbors might show up with guns and try to get in. They might even try to kill us—they might be that desperate. I imagined the Hillsingers and DeMarios and Scotts marching down Comanche Avenue carrying baseball bats and rifles— friends suddenly turned enemies, like in an episode of *The Twilight Zone*. "Your father will have a gun, too," said my mother. "To protect us with."

34 As time went by, the drop-drills and discreet lectures occurred less and less. One Halloween, I wanted to turn the bomb shelter into a haunted house—with spider webs, skeletons, and flying ghosts—but my father forbid it. For a while, he periodically changed the water and canned goods, and aired it out. Eventually, though, it just sat there in the middle of our backyard, a neglected reminder of my father's fear.

At the Glass Onion, 1971

He stood behind me while I played pinball
in a corner of the bar. He rubbed his
hard-on against my jeans. It was the fall
after the rape. Nineteen, I was a wiz

at the game, but as he ran his large hand
along the inside of my thighs and said
how much he wanted to take me home and
fuck me, I glanced up at the flashing red

and white lights and let my last ball slide past
the flippers. Instead of getting more change,
as I'd said, I bypassed the bar and dashed
into the bathroom. No lock, though. "You're strange,"

he said, tugging. I looked down at his head
till someone knocked, stuffed my wet cock, and fled.

4

Eighteen to Twenty-One

I

He said his name was Nick; later I learned
he'd crossed the country on stolen credit
cards—I found the receipts in the guest house
I rented for only three months. Over
a period of two weeks, he threatened
to tell my parents I was gay, blackmailed
me, tied me up, crawled through a window and
waited under my bed, and raped me at
knifepoint without lubricant. A neighbor
heard screams and called my parents, who arrived
with a loaded gun in my mother's purse.
But Nick was gone. I moved back home, began
therapy, and learned that the burning in
my rectum was gonorrhea, not nerves.

II

Our first date, Dick bought me dinner and played
"Moon River" (at my request) on his grand
piano. Soon after that, he moved to
San Diego, but drove up every week-
end to see me. We'd sleep at his "uncle"'s
quaint cottage in Benedict Canyon—part
of Jean Harlow's old estate. One night, Dick
spit out my cum in the bathroom sink; I
didn't ask why. The next morning, over
steak and eggs at Dupar's, Dick asked me to
think about San Diego, said he'd put
me through school. I liked him because he looked
like Sonny Bono, but sipped my coffee
and glanced away. Still, Dick picked up the bill.

III

More than anything, I wanted Charlie
to notice me. I spent one summer in
and around his swimming pool, talking to
his roommates, Rudy and Ned. All three of
them were from New York; I loved their stories
about the bars and baths, Fire Island, docks
after dark. I watched for Charlie, played board
games with Rudy and Ned, crashed on the couch.
Occasionally, Charlie came home with-
out a trick and I slipped into his bed
and slept next to him. Once, he rolled over
and kissed me—bourbon on his breath—and we
had sex at last. I was disappointed,
though: his dick was so small it didn't hurt.

IV

I made a list in my blue notebook: *Nick,
Dick, Charlie, Kevin, Howard, Tom.* . . . Kevin
had been the boyfriend of an overweight
girl I knew in high school. I spotted him
at a birthday bash—on a yacht—for an
eccentric blonde "starlet" who called herself
Countess Kerushka. Kevin and I left
together, ended up thrashing around
on his waterbed while his mother, who'd
just had a breakdown, slept in the next room.
Howard was Kevin's best friend. We went for
a drive one night, ended up parking. His
lips felt like sandpaper, and I couldn't
cum—but I added his name to the list.

V

Tom used spit for lubricant and fucked me
on the floor of his Volkswagen van while
his ex-lover (also named Tom) drove and
watched (I was sure) in the rearview mirror.
Another of his exes, Geraldo,
once cornered me in Tom's bathroom, kissed me
and asked: "What does he see in you?" At a
gay students' potluck, I refilled my wine
glass and watched Tom flirt with several other
men in the room. Outside, I paced, chain-smoked,
kicked a dent in his van and, when he came
looking for me, slugged him as hard as I
could. It was the end of the affair, but
only the beginning of my drinking.

VI

I ordered another wine cooler and
stared at his tight white pants—the outline of
his cock hung halfway down his thigh. After
a few more drinks, I asked him to dance to
"The First Time Ever I Saw Your Face." He
pressed himself against me and wrapped his arms
around my neck. I followed him to his
apartment but, once in bed, lost interest.
I told him I was hung up on someone.
As I got dressed, he said: "If you love him,
you should go to him." Instead, I drove back
to the bar, drank more, and picked up a blond
bodybuilder who, once we were in bed,
whispered "Give me your tongue"—which turned me off.

44

VII

As one young guy screwed another young guy
on the screen, the man sitting a couple
seats to my right—who'd been staring at me
for the longest time—slid over. He stared
a little longer, then leaned against me
and held a bottle of poppers to my
nose. When it wore off, he was rubbing my
crotch. Slowly, he unzipped my pants, pulled back
my underwear, lowered his head, licked some
pre-cum from the tip of my dick, and then
went down on it. As he sucked, he held the
bottle up. I took it, twisted the cap
off and sniffed, then looked up at the two guys
on the screen, then up at the black ceiling.

45

5

Cinnamon Toast

was my favorite:
two slices of Wonder
Bread (Remember
the red, yellow and blue
bubbles on the white bag?)
smothered with C & H
("the only pure cane")
sugar ("from Hawaii"),
then lightly sprinkled
with Schilling cinnamon.
It was best when
all the sugar dissolved
in the margarine ("It's
not nice to fool Mother
Nature!" Or was I wear-
ing the Imperial crown?),
preferably in little pools.
Sometimes we'd have
avocado (I'd smush up
the green wedges with my
fork and pour tons of
Morton salt on top—
I loved the little girl
with the umbrella) or
peanut butter toast
(had to drink plenty

of milk if the Skippy
was dry), but it was
always cinnamon (or
rather the buttery
sugar) that I craved.
On weekdays, my mother
either made eggs (with
Oscar Mayer bacon, Jimmy
Dean sausages, canned
corned beef hash or
Spam) or, if she was
rushed, set out several
boxes of breakfast cereal,
usually Wheaties, Special
K, grape-nuts, Corn Flakes,
Cheerios or Shredded Wheat—
all of which you had to add
sugar to. In the cereal
aisle at the supermarket,
I begged her to buy
the sweeter, more colorful
kinds: Froot Loops, Sugar
Crisp, Lucky Charms (with
those "magically delicious"
marshmallow bits: yellow
moons, pink hearts, green
clovers, orange stars),
Rice Krispies (which
crackled, but never seemed
to snap or pop), Cap'n
Crunch (with "crunch

berries"), Crispy Critters,
Alpha-Bits (I could never
find the right sugar-
frosted oat letters to
finish my soggy words),
Count Chocula, ("I'm
Cuckoo For") Cocoa Puffs,
Cocoa (or Fruity) Pebbles,
Cocoa Krispies, Frosted Flakes
("They're Gr-r-reat!"),
Honey-Comb, Apple Jacks,
Kix and Trix. I sympathized
with the silly rabbit on TV
commercials—he always
came so close to eating
the animated orange, lemon,
raspberry and grape-flavored
puffs, only to be foiled
by those snotty kids. Once,
I entered a "Should The
Rabbit Be Allowed To Eat
Trix?" contest by mailing
a postcard with my vote
to General Mills, and felt
personally responsible
when, due to an overwhelming
audience response, they
finally let the poor creature
taste a spoonful of the
stuff. (They never actually
gave him a whole bowl.)

I was forever saving box tops
and sending away for toys
(I waited weeks for a Tony
the Tiger detective kit) or
greedily digging in new boxes
of cereal for the advertised
prize: a plastic magnifying
glass, a Batman "Crime-
fighter" button, Flintstones
finger-puppets ("Collect
All Four!"), a ring with
a secret compartment, etc.
I tried, but failed, to
collect all the Welch's
Grape Jelly jars with
pictures of cartoon characters
(Casper the friendly ghost,
Mighty Mouse, Rocky & Bullwinkle,
Road Runner—"Beep! Beep!"—
& Wile E. Coyote—I didn't
learn his name till years
later) and super-heroes
(I made my mother buy me
the one with Wonder Woman
twirling her golden lasso
even though we had half
a dozen unopened jars
at home). It was like
magic: as soon as each
jar was empty, I'd wait
for the dishwasher to

rinse away the sticky
purple remains, and out
would come a steaming,
sparkling-clean Tom &
Jerry or Boris & Natasha
glass. Day after day,
however, as I drank
Ovaltine, Tang (just
like the astronauts!)
and Nestle Quik (the
chocolate or strawberry
powder always globbed when
I added milk), every one
of them (even Superman)
began to peel and fade.
On cold mornings, we had
Quaker Oats (Remember
the white-haired man on
the round carton?) or
Cream of Wheat (I liked
it lumpy, with clumps
of brown sugar, which,
as they melted, I'd
swirl with my spoon).
Later, after my mother
returned to work, we
had instant oatmeal or
pop-tarts (Blueberry,
Strawberry, Cherry,
Dutch Apple and—sheer
Heaven!—Frosted Chocolate

Fudge), which we could
grab from the toaster
and eat on the way to
school. On Saturdays,
my mother would sleep in
then fix us Aunt Jemima
pancakes (or sometimes
waffles or French toast).
I'd spread several pats
of butter between each
flapjack and pour maple
syrup (either Log Cabin
or Mrs. Butterworth's—
Remember her? A bottle
shaped like a lady!)

until it dripped down
the sides and surrounded
the whole stack like a moat.
Sunday mornings were the
worst. We couldn't have
anything (except water
and one glass of orange
juice) until after church.
It never failed—about
halfway through Mass
my stomach would start
to growl. I tried to
disguise it by coughing,
tried sucking it in to
make it stop. I'd sit
and stand when you were

supposed to, and pretend
to say the words, but
all I could think about
were the Winchell's donuts
my mother always treated
us to on the way home:
jelly-filled, glazed twists,
buttermilk, bear claws,
powdered fritters, cinnamon
spice and (my favorites)
the ones with different-
colored icing: white with
shredded coconut, orange
with chocolate specks, pink
with chopped pecans, yellow
with red, green and blue
sprinkles. After receiving
Communion, I'd kneel in
the pew and wait an eternity
for that wafer (God, how I
wanted to chew it!) to dissolve
on the roof of my mouth.

The Ten Best Episodes of *The Patty Duke Show*

1. Patty cheats on a computerized intelligence test and is pronounced a genius.

2. Ross blackmails Patty and Cathy by tape recording their conversation at a slumber party.

3. Patty is cast as Cleopatra in the school play, but gets stage fright on opening night.

4. Patty writes a novel entitled *I Was a Teenage Teenager.*

5. Cathy wears Patty's expensive new dress to a piano concert and accidentally spills punch on it.

6. Patty and Cathy run against each other for class president.

7. Frankie Avalon's car breaks down in front of the Lane house.

8. Patty raffles a date with Richard for the church bazaar, then gets jealous and tries to buy all the tickets back.

9. Patty's tonsils are taken out by a dreamboat doctor (played by Troy Donahue).

10. Patty pretends to be Cathy and flirts with Richard to see if he'll be faithful to her.

Answer Song

for Tim Dlugos

Lesley Gore got her rival good
in the smash answer to "It's My Party,"
"Judy's Turn To Cry," when her
unfaithful boyfriend, Johnny, suddenly
came to his senses in the midst
of yet another apparently unchaperoned shindig.
I picture Judy—hot pink mini-dress
and ratted black hair—being swept away
by a flood of her own teenage tears.
In triumph, Lesley rehangs Johnny's ring
around her neck. She has no idea that
the British are coming, that her popularity
will wane and she'll watch her hits drop
off the charts like so many tinkling
heart-shaped charms, and that there she'll be:
a has-been at seventeen. Naturally
she'll finish high school and marry
Johnny. They'll have a couple of kids
and settle down in a yellow two-story
tract house with white-shuttered windows
and bright red flower beds. At the supermart,
Lesley will fill her cart with frozen dinners,
which she'll serve with a smile as the family
gathers round their first color TV.
Week after week, she'll exchange recipes,
attend PTA meetings and Tupperware parties,

usher Brownie troops past tar pits
and towering dinosaur bones. Whenever
she hears one of her songs on an oldie station,
she'll think about those extinct beasts.
She'll think about them too as, year
after year, she tosses headlines
into the trash: Vietnam, Nixon, Patty Hearst.
Then one afternoon—her children grown
and gone—she'll discover a strange
pair of earrings in the breast pocket
of Johnny's business suit. It's downhill
after that: curlers, migraines, fattening
midnight snacks. Or is it? She did,
after all, sing "You Don't Own Me,"
the first pop song with a feminist twist.

What if Lesley hears about women's lib?
What if she goes into therapy and begins
to question her attraction to emotionally
unavailable men? Suppose, under hypnosis,
she returns to her sixteenth birthday party,
relives all those tears, and learns that
it was Judy—not Johnny—she'd wanted
all along. There's no answer to that
song, of course, but I have
heard rumors.

It's Not Unusual

My platinum blonde hair

held in place

by a paisley scarf

as I speed down

Route 66

in the pink convertible

I won

behind Door Number 3

Yvette Mimieux in *Hit Lady*

All I remember is she drives a red
sports car and wears an ankh around her neck
and is instructed by The Company
to bump off some union bigwig because
he's scheduled to testify against a
Mafioso so she assumes a new
identity and starts dating him and
naturally he falls madly in love
with her not suspecting that this pert blonde
sitting on the other side of the pink
roses at the fancy restaurant is
actually the best assassin in
the business but when the time comes to pull
the trigger she breaks out in a cold sweat
and can't go through with it because all she
really wants is to quit The Company
and marry her struggling artist boyfriend
who's played by Dack Rambo and who of course
has no idea she kills people for a
living so she slips away and puts her
silencer in a storage locker at
the airport and flies to this picturesque
seaside village in Mexico where Dack
paints his unsalable masterpieces
and hoping to make a fresh start she tells
him everything but it turns out that Dack
works for The Company too so he shoots
her in the back on the beach and she dies.

Three Deaths

First there was Joanne (I can't remember her last name), a classmate of mine at Superior Street Elementary School. She was killed in a traffic accident—along with the driver and a dozen other kids, including the daughter of Roy Rogers and Dale Evans—on the way back from a Christian picnic. The bus hit a car, went out of control, and ran off a freeway overpass. Joanne and I sat next to each other in Mrs. Fields' first grade class. She was always teased about being a tomboy; during recess, she kicked balls while, in a corner of the playground, I jumped rope with the girls. At home, I saw the crushed, upside-down church bus on television, and heard words like "tragedy" and "celebrity" for the first time. My mother tried to explain it all to me. The next morning, someone put flowers on Joanne's empty chair. I remember staring at the aluminum foil wrapped around the stems.

Then there was Lee Ann Tate. She lived in the cul-de-sac that faced our house on Comanche Avenue. We used to get into terrible fights—I forget about what. She had younger twin brothers, both brats. One summer, my brother and a few of his friends from the neighborhood lured Lee Ann into a tent in our backyard and stuck a Barbie leg up her vagina. They bragged about it for weeks afterwards. The Tates had long since moved to Simi Valley when my mother handed me an article from *The Green Sheet* that said Lee

Ann (eighteen) had died in a small boat that capsized off Catalina. Lee Ann and four young men—one of them her boyfriend? her fiancé? There was a picture of the rescue team laying out the bodies on the beach. I saved the clipping for a while, then threw it away.

Kathe Lindsay, who lived down the block, made it to thirty-three, which surprised everybody. When we were in junior high, they discovered a malignant tumor the size of a baseball in her uterus. That phrase was repeated a lot: "the size of a baseball." From then on, she was in and out of hospitals, but kept living, and was eventually able to lead (according to updates from my mother) a "normal" life. Kathe even got married, but couldn't—everyone commented—have kids. Years later, I attended her funeral, waited in a long line to give my condolences to her parents. Mr. Lindsay didn't recognize me; Mrs. Lindsay—Kathleen—did. We talked for a few seconds. I said something like: "I wish I could have known her better." Kathleen looked at me blankly, then turned to greet the next person in line.

Pacoima, California, 1956

Mother was vacuuming the family room.
I sat watching black-and-white cartoons on
the small-screened tv. There was a loud boom;
the house shook. She dragged me out on the lawn

where May, our neighbor, pointed. A gray cloud
billowed above the roofs on the next block.
I remember being pulled through a crowd
in front of the grammar school. All the smoke

came from across the street. Black ashes swirled
around like snowflakes. The tail of the plane
was in flames on the high school football field.
May found my brother clinging to a chain-

link fence, his face red with tears. Mother cried
too, and bent down as the big trucks arrived.

6

V.O.D.

Things to Do in *Valley of the Dolls* (The Movie)

Move to New York.
Lose your virginity.
Become a star.
Send money to your mother.

Call pills "dolls."
Fire the talented newcomer.
Have a nervous breakdown.
Suffer from an incurable degenerative disease.

Sing the theme song.
Do your first nude scene.
Wear gowns designed by Travilla.
Become addicted to booze and dope.

Scream "Who needs you!"
Stagger around in a half-slip and bra.
Come to in a sleazy hotel room.
Say "I am merely traveling incognito."

Get drummed out of Hollywood.
Come crawling back to Broadway.
Pull off Susan Hayward's wig
and try to flush it down the toilet.

End up in a sanitarium.
Hiss "It wasn't a nuthouse!"
Get an abortion.
Go on a binge.

Detect a lump in your breast.
Commit suicide.
Make a comeback.
Overact.

It's a Wig!

Neely unzipped her dress and let it fall to the floor. Christ, she was tired. And it was late. She squinted at the clock in the hallway. Eleven-thirty! Shit! Ted had made her swear she'd be home for dinner—and she'd blown it! He was probably upstairs, fast asleep by now. She stood there for a second, fuming about her day at the studio. It had been pure hell. Sure, she'd taken a few dolls before filming began, but those cameramen—they'd tried to fry her alive! "It's too hot!" she remembered shouting. "It's too damn hot!" The rest was a big blur. She vaguely recalled something about . . . a wiglet! That's right! She'd yanked off her wiglet and thrown it at the assistant director. Then she'd walked off the set. "Oh, God!" she moaned. At this rate, they'd never complete the fucking picture. Just thinking about it made her head ache. "Screw the picture!" she slurred. Those bastards would never learn how to treat talent like hers. She stepped over her dress and stumbled across the living room.

At the bar, she fumbled for a bottle of scotch. "Just one little drinkie," she promised herself, raising the bottle. The alcohol went down like warm oil. Neely smacked her lips. "Just what the little ol' doctor ordered." While taking a second swig, she heard a splash. Jesus! Who in hell was in the pool? She peered through the patio door. It was dark, but the cabana lights were on, and their reflection hit the water. Ted! Just then, someone jumped in and paddled towards him. Neely pressed her nose against the glass. It was...some...WHORE! Ted usually fooled around with boys—*that* she had learned to accept. But this? A girl? Her mind reeled. This was it! Banging some bimbo in her own swimming pool! This was the last fucking straw!

Neely pulled open the door. She recognized Ted's voice: "It's not cold, huh?" "What if she hears us?" the girl asked timidly. "Oh relax, baby," he laughed. "By this time she's so full of pills and booze an earthquake couldn't rouse her."

Neely felt sick to her stomach. She groped her way to the switch and triumphantly flooded the pool with light. Then, in her bra, half-slip, and white high-heeled pumps, she staggered outside, still clutching the bottle of scotch. "Having fun, kiddies?" Ted and the girl scrambled out of the water. "Don't mind me, go right ahead!" she screamed. "I'll watch!" Frantically, the girl dodged behind Ted. "You'd better hide, you little tramp! How dare you contaminate my pool!"

Neely lurched forward. She held up the bottle and, sneering at the shivering couple, emptied all the scotch into the swimming pool. "Here!" she hissed. "Maybe this'll disinfect it!"

•

PATTY:	Here, Cath, try this. It's great for swelling.
MRS. LANE:	*(entering bedroom)* Here's your dress, dear. I ironed it and...Oh, haven't you two started to get ready yet? *(She looks at her wristwatch.)* Your guests will be arriving soon. Cathy, what's the matter with your arm?
CATHY:	Nothing, Aunt Natalie.
MRS. LANE:	Well then why have you got a hot-water bot—
PATTY:	*(interrupting)* Mom, I have a confession to make. I didn't get my flu shot. Cathy did.
MRS. LANE:	What?
CATHY:	It was an accident. I went in to tell the doctor that Patty was there and he thought I was Patty and before I knew it...Ouch!
MRS. LANE:	Oh, you poor baby!
CATHY:	*(starting to sit up)* I'm fine. Really.
MRS. LANE:	No, you stay in bed.
CATHY:	But I have to get dressed for the party.
MRS. LANE:	I'm afraid there's not going to be any party for you tonight. I'm going to go call Dr. Williams. *(She leaves room.)*
CATHY:	Oh, Patty.
PATTY:	I know how you feel, Cath. *(She walks around and sits on her twin bed.)* I'll tell you what. If you can't come down to the party, I won't either.

CATHY:	You won't?
PATTY:	Well...uh...sure. Of course. If that's what you want me to do. *(Pause)* Do you?
CATHY:	No.
PATTY:	You talked me out of it. *(laugh track)* For your sake, I'll go down. But I won't have a good time.
CATHY:	You'd better call Ted and tell him. He was looking forward to the dance contest.
PATTY:	Why don't we wait. Maybe the doctor will say it's all right.

•

Neely pushed her hair out of her face and gestured for the bartender to refill her shot glass. Then she unclasped her purse and searched for her pills. "A blue doll'll do the trick," she thought. "A beautiful little blue jewel." Excitedly, she popped the lid off a prescription bottle and poured three or four capsules into the palm of her hand. She gulped them down. Her initial feeling of relief, however, faded as she caught a glimpse of herself in the mirror across the bar. Her hair was all scraggly, and she looked bloated and tired.

Ever since she won her Oscar, nothing had gone right. Ted had left her for a Beverly Hills interior decorator. Her last picture had flopped, and she'd been fired from her new one—"uncooperative" the studio memo had said. And now Lyon and Anne were trying to convince her to check into a sanitarium. Under the circumstances, she'd done the only sensible thing: gotten on the first plane out of Hollywood. And here she was, slumped at the bar in this dingy San Francisco dive.

As she lit a cigarette, one of her old hits came on the jukebox. She tried to sing along with herself, but her voice was hoarse and she could barely remember the lyrics. "Whatcha say? Huh?" Some old drunk was pawing at her arm. She pulled away. Why was San Francisco full of so many freaks? "Whatcha say, baby?" Neely spun around. "Whadaya mean 'baby'?" she snarled. "I'm Neely O'Hara, pal. That's *me* singing on that jukebox." The drunk laughed. "What're ya, kiddin'? Listen, that dame's great. You sound like a frog!" He laughed at her again. "Like a frog!" Neely grabbed her shot glass and threw the scotch in the drunk's face. For an instant, he looked shocked; then he turned red with rage and lunged at her, clutching his hands around her neck.

"Take it easy, buddy," she heard the bartender say. "She's stoned." A few of the other customers had managed to pull the guy off of her. Neely straightened up and brushed herself off. "Who's stoned?" she demanded. "I am merely traveling incognito." She put on a pair of sunglasses and looked around haughtily. "Well, get outta here, will ya!" yelled the drunk who had attacked her. "Go on, get outta here!"

Neely slid off the barstool and bumped into the jukebox, which was still playing her song as she tottered toward the door.

•

On the set of her TV show, Patty Duke had two separate dressing rooms. Both were adorned with a personalized silver star—one for Patty, the typical American teenager, and one for Cathy, her demure, intellectual identical cousin. It was simply a publicity gimmick. No one at ABC actually expected Patty to use two dressing rooms, so they had failed to install a connecting door. Nevertheless, Ethel Ross insisted she use both of them. This was a real hardship for Patty: she was always leaving in one room something that she needed in the other. Whenever Patty complained, Ethel would light a Salem, staining the white filter with red lipstick, and glare at the young star as she breathed out a stream of smoke. "I like it. It's cute. Use both."

Despite her confidence in front of a camera, Patty was basically shy. Every time there was a character change, she would have to enter one dressing room, take off her costume, slip into a thin robe, and walk back out in the hall in order to enter the other dressing room. Members of the crew were always milling about; they'd eye her as she passed between the Patty room and the Cathy room. Humiliated, Patty would clutch the collar of her robe and stare down at her bare feet.

•

NEELY: *(voiceover)* At first it was awful . . . like living in a zoo. They stuck me in this cheesy little bedroom and this big ugly nurse with orthopedic shoes never left my side. I asked for a cigarette:

> NEELY: *(scowling)* Gimme a cigarette!

> NURSE: Two a day. During social hour.

I told her I had no intention of socializing with kooks. I couldn't sleep; I needed a pill. I started screaming. I figured they'd give me something to calm me. They sure did:

> NEELY: *(wrestling with two nurses)* Let go of me, you! Let go of me!

They ordered me to take off my nightgown. I told 'em to drop dead. They took it off for me:

> NEELY: *(her white hospital shift being pulled over her head)* No!

Then they stuck me in this big tub and hooked a canvas around me. And this young nurse sat there and wrote down everything I said. I used words that sure aren't in medical books:

> NEELY: *(her head sticking out of canvas tub cover, wildly shaking her hair)* You stupid ass nurse! What are you looking at?

Actually, the water felt great. It kept coming in and going out. I wanted to lie back and relax, but that was what *they* wanted. I tore this small hole in the canvas and I started working at it with my big toe. Pretty soon I got half my foot through it. Then I yanked my knee up to my chest:

(*Sound of canvas ripping*)

NEELY: (*in agony*) Ow! Ow! God! It hurts!

The nurse sounded the alarm:

(*Sound of alarm*)

•

(*Patty and Cathy sit on their twin beds. Patty switches off her portable hair dryer as Mrs. Lane enters room.*)

MRS. LANE:	(*to Cathy*) I just spoke to the doctor. He says you're having a mild reaction to the shot. It happens occasionally. It's nothing to worry about. You stay in bed tonight and you'll be fine in the morning.
CATHY:	(*rising*) I'm sure I'll be all right.
MRS. LANE:	You stay in bed, young lady. (*She smiles lovingly.*) Oh, I know it's a disappointment, but there'll be other parties. I'll get you an ice pack. (*She glances at Patty.*) The doctor said to apply *cold* to the arm. (*She leaves room.*)
PATTY:	(*shrugging her shoulders*) So I'm not Ben Casey. (*laugh track*)

•

In her study, Jackie slipped a piece of pink paper into her manual typewriter. As was her habit, she wrote five drafts of a book, each one on different-colored paper (yellow, pink, green, blue, and white, in that order), before submitting it to her publisher. With both index fingers, she started tapping out a paragraph from a yellow draft. *Neely closed the script wearily. No use going over it again. She knew it cold. She stretched luxuriously in the large bed and sipped some scotch.* Jackie stopped. Should she capitalize "scotch"? She bit at the end of a pen and thought for a moment. Yes, she finally decided, she liked it big. She backspaced and struck a large "s" over the small one. "Voilà!" she exclaimed happily to her poodle Josephine, who was asleep at her feet. Quickly she typed: *Maybe she should take another doll. She had already taken two . . . maybe another red one.* Instinctively, Jackie paused. Something was missing. But what? Suddenly it hit her. She should mention the time, let the reader know that the scene takes place at night. She looked up at the clock: eleven-thirty. She backspaced again and x-ed out the sentences she'd just typed. Christ, writing was time-consuming! Eleven-thirty! She'd worked nonstop since dinner! She knew she was pushing herself too hard, but she wanted to fine-tune this paragraph before turning in. As usual, Irving was already in bed, watching TV; she could hear a faint burst of *Tonight Show* applause on the other side of their apartment.

Lost in thought, Jackie automatically fondled her left breast. "Shit!" She'd been worried about the lump she discovered last week. She meant to call the doctor earlier that day, but had been absorbed in her book. "Tomorrow," she reminded herself. "I must make an appointment tomorrow."

She looked down at the pink page and felt a surge of determination. *Eleven-thirty and she was still wide awake. Maybe she should take another doll. She had already taken two . . . maybe another red one. She had to be on the set at six. She wandered into the bathroom and popped a red pill into her mouth.* "Come on, you little doll, do the job."

Jackie sat back and smiled with satisfaction. Sometimes— she didn't know how or why—her writing was so inspired. She stretched her arms, then switched off the desk lamp. "You're beautiful, kiddo," she said, nudging Josephine with her foot. "Let's call it a night."

•

"You *will* make a guest appearance at the Cystic Fibrosis benefit." Ethel lit a Salem and clicked her gold lighter shut. They were alone in the Cathy room. "Fuck you!" snapped Patty as she ripped off her prim schoolgirl blouse. It landed on the floor, next to her pageboy wig. Ethel glared. Patty stuck out her tongue. "We'll see what John has to say about this." Ethel stood up, marched to the door, and slammed it behind her. Patty threw on her robe, stormed out of the Cathy room, made a nasty face at one of the crew members in the hall, and pushed open the door to the Patty room with the palms of both hands.

Once she had changed into her sock-hop outfit, she sat at the vanity and dabbed her tears with a pink Kleenex. She stared at herself in the mirror. "*I* am an Academy Award-winning star," she said out loud. The thought of her Oscar filled her with rage. She grabbed a bottle of cold cream and hurled it at the wall. Ethel had made her wear that hideous mint-green dress! And she was photographed with Joan Crawford—a great star! She had to stand next to Miss Crawford—who looked so elegant in her beautiful beaded gown—and smile and hold up her Oscar wearing that hideous, ugly, awful mint-green dress!!! More bottles shattered against the walls of the Patty room.

Patty cringed remembering how Ethel had insisted on bringing her decrepit chihuahua Bambi to the awards ceremony. In fact, that dog was better dressed than Patty was! Ethel made Bambi a little silk dress and a little mink stole and carried her all around the Santa Monica Civic Auditorium in a pyramid-shaped black leather bag! God, Patty hated that dog! All those years of trying to get it to eat, standing there forever holding out that plate of gray gruel and repeating, in a screechy voice (which, according to Ethel, was a high enough pitch for the dog to hear): "Does Bambi want her dinner?" Or trying to get the stupid thing to pee, asking it, in that same high-pitched screechy voice: "Does Bambi want to make a river?" "Does Bambi want her dinner?" "Does Bambi want to make a river?" The Rosses had always been nicer to the fucking dog than they were to her. And *she* was the one who paid all the bills! *She* was the youngest person ever to win an Academy Award! Oh God, that was the worst night of her whole goddamn life!

One by one, Patty pulled all the tissues out of the Kleenex dispenser, squeezed them into a big ball, and threw them at herself in the vanity mirror.

After a while, she calmed down enough to pull on her Patty wig—a puffy brunette flip—and clip a pink velvet bow just above the bangs.

•

Neely followed Helen Lawson into the powder room. Though she'd become a star on her own, Neely had never forgiven Helen for firing her from her Broadway show so many years ago. Granted, Neely had had her ups and downs. Her stay in the sanitarium, for instance—what a low point *that* little incident was! God, how she'd fought to keep it out of the papers! But all of that was behind her now. She was making her comeback—in a musical produced by David Merrick! She was on top again—bigger and better than ever! Helen's career, on the other hand, had begun to fizzle out—and fast. She was losing her looks, her voice, her fans. And her new show had just gotten terrible notices in Philly. Neely wasn't about to let this opportunity pass.

Helen sat in front of one of the mirrors, brushing her thick red hair. She wore a gold beaded pantsuit and a green organdy scarf, tucked in at the neck. Neely walked past her slowly, like a predator stalking its prey. She slipped off her satin dinner coat, revealing a pleated white Empire evening gown. Clusters of white beads hung from her ears. She stood in front of the mirror next to Helen and opened her handbag, eyeing the aging star as she pulled out her compact. "Who're you hiding from, Helen?" she said tauntingly. "The notices couldn't've been that bad." Helen lit a cigarette and spoke as she exhaled smoke. "The show just needs a little doctoring." "Don't worry, sweetheart," mocked Neely. "If it flops, I can always get you a job as understudy—for my grandmother." "Thanks," Helen retorted. "I've already turned down the part you're playin'." "Bull!" snapped Neely. "Merrick's not *that* crazy." "You should know, honey," countered Helen. "*You* just came out of the nuthouse." "It was *not* a nuthouse," Neely hissed. Hearing the two celebrities exchange insults, the powder-room attendant meekly ducked out of sight.

"Look," said Helen, pointing her burning cigarette at Neely. "They drummed you right out of Hollywood. So you come crawling back to Broadway. Well, Broadway doesn't go for *booze* and *dope*. Now get out of my way," she ordered, abruptly standing up. "I've got a *man* waitin' for me." Neely blocked her exit and laughed derisively. "That's a switch from the *fags* you're usually stuck with!" "At least I never married one!" Helen replied sharply. She shoved past Neely and headed for the door. "You take that back, you old bag!" Neely leaped after Helen and grabbed her by the hair. "Get your hands off me!" Helen jerked away. Suddenly Neely let out a gasp of amazement. She stood staring at the thing in her hands. At the same time, Helen's hands flew up to her head in horror. Her real hair was short, ragged, and completely gray.

"Oh, my God!" squealed Neely, holding it up. "IT'S A WIG!" "Gimme back my hair, you little bitch!" Helen reached out, but Neely jumped back. She waved the wig like a flag. "Her hair's as phony as she is!" "Gimme that!" Neely put it on and danced around the room. "Hey! Dig me as a redhead!" Helen chased after her. "Gimme that, damn you!"

Neely dashed into one of the enclosed toilets and bolted the door. Frantically, Helen pounded on the stall. "What the hell are you doing in there?" "Giving it a shampoo," giggled Neely. "Goodbye, pussycat. Meeee-ow." She dropped the wig in the toilet and flushed. "God, she's throwing it in the can!" cried Helen. "I'll kill 'er!" Inside, Neely gingerly held up the sopping wet wig. It had shrunk significantly, and was dripping like a drenched animal. "How do you like that—it won't even go down the john." "Gimme that wig!" By now, Helen was hysterical. "OK," Neely said scornfully. "You want it back? Here it comes—" She tossed it over the top of the stall door. "Special Delivery!"

With a splat, the wig landed on the powder-room floor.

•

After dinner, Jackie and Irving went home to their apartment and took sleeping pills, then went to bed with the television on. Johnny Carson was interviewing Truman Capote, and as Jackie listened, half asleep, she suddenly realized that Capote was talking about her. She heard him say: "She looks like a truck driver in drag."

Jackie tried to wake Irving, who had succumbed to the sleeping pills, and finally had to pour water on him to get his attention. She told him about Capote's insults, which had included the opinion that she was "a born transvestite" who wears "sleazy wigs and gowns."

Irving was outraged, but Jackie was deeply hurt. Why was she always getting attacked on talk shows? Gore, Truman, Norman—those guys were out to crucify her. "Pretentious literary types," she thought. "They're just jealous of my sales." Hadn't the *Guinness Book of World Records* credited *V.O.D.* as the best-selling novel of all time? Damn right. Wasn't Shakespeare the soap opera king of his day? You betcha. Hadn't her new book, *The Love Machine*, shot up the bestseller lists at breakneck speed? Yes, indeed. Wasn't it selling like hotcakes? Indeed, indeed. In-dee-dee. "That's our girl," she reassured herself as the sleeping pills finally kicked in. "We're *it*. We're Number One."

A month after Capote made his malicious remarks, Jackie appeared on Johnny Carson's show. By then, Jackie's "literary" feud with Capote had received tons of press. She wore her biggest black wig and her most psychedelic Pucci outfit. Her fingers were loaded with gold rings, including a large ankh symbol. An even larger ankh hung from a chain around her neck. Surprisingly, Jackie made no mention of

Capote during her chat with Johnny. At last, Carson asked the question that was on everyone's mind: "What do you think of Truman?"

Jackie considered this for a second, then answered: "Truman? I think history will prove he was one of the best Presidents we've had." Her coy smile quickly broadened. The audience erupted with laughter and applause, and Jackie soaked it up.

After the taping, Irving's limousine rushed her to her chemotherapy appointment at Doctors Hospital.

•

84 CATHY: I can't stand Ted up at the last minute. He'll never date me again. Never.

PATTY: I wish I could change places with you so that you could go to the party and I could . . . *(Pause)* I can keep your date with Ted!

CATHY: What?

PATTY: He'll think it's you!

CATHY: You couldn't.

PATTY: Of course I could! You took my shot for me, the least I can do is date your boyfriend for you. *(laugh track: chuckles)* It's better than having him bring another girl. This way we'll keep him in the family.

CATHY: What about your date with Richard?

PATTY: I'll keep that, too.

CATHY: You can't be both of us. When the boys come, there have to be two of us.

PATTY: You've got a point. Let me think. There are two boys coming over for two girls...

CATHY: And there's only one of you.

PATTY: Is there? *(imitating Cathy)* Good evening, Ted old chap. You're looking simply divine this evening.

CATHY: I don't talk like that.

PATTY: That's what you think.

CATHY: How can you fool both of them?

PATTY: Leave it to me.

CATHY: Patty, promise me one thing?

PATTY: What?

CATHY: You can kiss your date, but not mine. Promise?

PATTY: Promise. Gee, I hope I don't get confused.

●

Neely looked up at the unlit marquee. The words were blurred, but she managed to make out the two at the bottom: OPENING NIGHT. Bewildered, she glanced around. The theater was dark, the street deserted. "Hey! Where is everybody?" she shouted. "Hey, everybody! Where are you?" Her voice trailed off. "Where are you?"

Suddenly, it all came back. She'd hidden a bottle of scotch in her makeup case, and gotten drunk in her dressing room.

They'd attempted to sober her up, but she had been too belligerent. At the last minute, those sons of bitches had called in her understudy. A goddamn understudy—on *her* opening night! "You're not stealing *my* part, sister!" she'd shrieked, furiously trying to choke the little opportunist. It had taken several stagehands to pry Neely from her replacement and carry her, kicking and screaming, out through the rear of the theater. She'd ended up spending the evening in the bar across the street, popping dolls with shots of alcohol.

Neely reeled into the alley and pounded on the stage door. "Gone," she mumbled. "Everybody's gone." She staggered backwards, gesturing angrily. "The hell with 'em! Who needs 'em! The whole world loves me!!!" She leaned against a trash can and hung her head. "Oh, God," she whimpered. "God, God, God…" Slowly, she lifted her tear-streaked face and raised both arms, like a child grabbing at something out of reach. "God?" The silence frightened her. She hugged herself and rocked back and forth. "Oh, Neely…Neely, Neely, Neely…NEELY O'HARA!!!" Then she collapsed, her small body heaving with sobs, clenched fists beating the asphalt.

"My dolls, my beautiful, beautiful dolls!"

The Shower Scene in *Psycho*

She closes the bathroom door to secure her privacy, slips off her robe, drapes it over the toilet bowl, steps into the bath, and closes the shower curtain behind her, filling the frame with a flash of white (5.89).

Shortly before midnight on Friday, August 8, 1969, Manson called together Family members Tex Watson, Susan Atkins, Patricia Krenwinkel, and Linda Kasabian to give them their instructions.

From Marion viewed through the translucent shower curtain, Hitchcock cuts to (5.90), framed from within the space bounded by the curtain. At the top center of this frame is the shower head.

Fortified with drugs and armed with a gun, knives, rope, and wire cutters, they were to take one of the Family cars and go to 10050 Cielo Drive in Beverly Hills.

Marion rises into the frame. Water begins to stream from the shower head. She looks up into the stream of water and begins to wash her neck and arms. Her expression is ecstatic as the water brings her body to life (5.91).

In the secluded ranch-style house at the end of the cul-de-sac, Sharon Tate, aged twenty-six, a star of *Valley of the Dolls* and now eight and a half months pregnant, was entertaining three guests: Hollywood hair stylist Jay Sebring, coffee heiress Abigail Folger, and Folger's lover Voytek Frykowski.

At this point, there is a cut to Marion's vision of the shower head, water radiating from it in all directions like a sunburst (5.92).

(I had just turned sixteen, was about to start my last year at Chatsworth High.)

Hitchcock cuts to the shower head viewed from the side (5.93) at the precise moment Marion turns her naked back to the stream of water.

(Every Saturday, I went to the matinee at the Chatsworth Cinema.)

Marion takes pleasure in the stream of water emanating from the shower head (5.94).

(The theater was next to the Thrifty Drug where, two summers before, I'd bought a copy of *Valley of the Dolls*.)

From the side view of the shower head, Hitchcock cuts back to Marion, still ecstatic (5.95). Then he cuts to a setup that places the camera where the tile wall of the shower "really" is.

(I took it home and hid it under my bed. I knew it was the kind of book my mother wouldn't let me read.)

The shower curtain, to which Marion's back is turned, hangs from a bar at the top of the screen, and forms a frame-within-a-frame that almost completely fills the screen (5.96).

(The summer before that, she'd found the box of newspaper clippings on the top shelf of my closet.)

The camera begins to move forward, until the bar at the top becomes excluded from the screen (5.97).

(For weeks, I'd been cutting out articles about murders.)

Synchronized with this movement of the camera, Marion slides out of the frame, so that the shower curtain completely fills the screen (5.98).

(It started with the eight nurses in Chicago. Right after that was the Texas sniper. Then there was the politician's daughter who was bludgeoned and stabbed to death in her sleep.)

A shadowy figure, barely visible through the shower curtain, enters the door that can just be made out in the background. It steps forward toward the camera, its form doubled by and blending into its shadow cast on the translucent curtain (5.99).

After cutting telephone wires to the house, they gained access to the property by scaling fences, careful not to set off alarms.

The curtain is suddenly wrenched open and a silhouetted knife-wielding figure is revealed (5.100).

As they walked up the drive, a car approached from the house and caught them in its headlights.

The silhouetted figure is symmetrically flanked by the raised knife on the one side and the light bulb on the other (5.101).

At the wheel was eighteen-year-old Steven Parent, who had been visiting the caretaker, William Garretson. In his apartment over the garage, Garretson listened to his stereo with headphones on, unaware of what was happening just yards away.

When the camera reverses field to Marion, turned away (5.102), her figure displaces the silhouette in (5.101).

Parent slowed down and asked who they were, and what they wanted.

It is through the silhouetted figure's eyes that Marion is now viewed, as she turns around clockwise until she looks right into the camera (5.103). What she sees makes her open her mouth to scream.

Watson's response was to place the barrel of a .22 against the youth's head and blast off four rounds.

Jump cut to a closer view of Marion's face (5.104).

(I didn't know why I was so fascinated by murder.)

Second jump cut to an extreme closeup of her wide-open mouth (5.105).

(I told my mother the clippings were "research," that one day I wanted to write about crime. She made me throw them away.)

From Marion's point of view, the silhouetted figure strikes out violently with its knife (5.106).

Watson slit one of the window-screens, crawled into the house, and admitted the others through the front door. Linda Kasabian remained outside as lookout.

The knife slashes down for the first time (5.107).

Frykowski, who was asleep on a sofa in the living room, woke up to find Watson standing over him, gun in hand.

The knife slashes through the corner of the screen. The arm and the knife remain silhouetted (5.108).

Atkins reported to Watson that there were three more people in the house. He ordered her to bring them into the living room, which she did at knife-point.

In a slightly closer variant of (5.107), the knife is again raised, its blade gleaming in the light.

(The first time I saw *Psycho*, I was baby-sitting for a couple who lived at the end of a dark cul-de-sac.)

This shot frames part of Marion's body along with the intruder's arm, still shadowy in the frame (5.109).

(I prayed they'd stay out late. I wouldn't have been allowed to watch it at home.)

Viewed from overhead, the shower-curtain bar cuts across the screen. As Marion tries to fend it off, the knife strikes three times (5.110).

(There was a storm that night: rain and branches beat against the windows. I waited anxiously for "The Late Show" to come on.)

Marion's face fills the screen, expressing bewilderment and pain (5.111).

(They'd cut most of the shower scene for TV.)

Marion holds onto the shadowy arm as it weaves three times in a spiraling movement (5.112).

(I felt cheated.)

Reprise of (5.111).

(I wanted to be scared.)

Reprise of (5.112).

When Sebring was told to lie face down on the floor, he tried to grab Watson's gun, whereupon Watson shot him through the lung.

Another variant of (5.107). The knife again slashes down.

Watson looped one end of a nylon rope around Sebring's neck, threw the free end over a beam and tied it around the necks of Folger and Tate, who had to stand upright to avoid being choked.

Marion turns her face away, her head almost sliding out of the frame (5.113).

Watson ordered Atkins to stab Frykowski, who got to his feet and ran outside. Atkins pursued him onto the lawn, and knifed him in the back.

The slashing knife (5.114).

Watson followed, shot Frykowski twice and, when his gun jammed, continued to beat him over the head with the butt.

A shot of Marion recoiling, still bewildered (5.115).

In the living room, the two women struggled to free themselves from their dual noose.

This shot approximates (5.114), but this time the knife slashes through the center of the frame.

93

Like Frykowski, Folger got as far as the front lawn. She was chased down by Krenwinkel, who stabbed her repeatedly.

Reprise of (5.115). Marion's bewildered reaction.

Watson also descended upon her, after first knifing Sebring.

The hand and knife come into clear focus. Water bounces off the glinting metal of the blade (5.116).

Then they turned on the heavily pregnant Miss Tate.

Juxtaposition of blade and flesh (5.117).

(In secret, I read *Valley of the Dolls* several times.)

Marion recoils, but still looks dazed, entranced (5.118).

(My mother found my hiding place and made me throw the book away.)

A low-angle view facing the door. The knife slashes through the frame (5.119).

(I bicycled to Thrifty Drug, bought another copy, and snuck it into the house.)

Marion's back and arms. The intruder's arm again enters the frame (5.120).

Watson told Atkins to stab her.

Closeup of Marion's face. She is now clearly in agony (5.121).

When the actress begged to be spared for the sake of her unborn child, Atkins sneered, "Look, bitch, I don't care…"

Blood drips down Marion's writhing legs (5.122).

"I have no mercy for you."

Marion turns her face from the camera. The knife enters the frame (5.123).

She hesitated nonetheless, so Watson inflicted the first wound.

Reprise of (5.122), with a greater flow of blood.

Within moments, Atkins and Krenwinkel joined in, stabbing her sixteen times.

The screen flashes white as the camera momentarily frames only the bare tile wall. Marion's hand, viewed from up close and out of focus, enters and then exits the frame (5.124).

Finally, Susan Atkins dipped a towel in Sharon Tate's blood and wrote the word "Pig" on the front door.

The intruder exits (5.125).

It was not until the next day, when they watched TV at the Spahn Movie Ranch in Chatsworth, that any of them knew who they had murdered.

Marion's hand pressed against the white tile (5.126). It slowly slides down the wall.

(The same summer I read *Valley of the Dolls*, the book was being made into a movie.)

Marion's hand drops out of the frame and her body slowly slides down the wall. She turns to face forward as her back slips down, the camera tilting down with her (5.127).

(After Patty Duke, my childhood idol, was cast in one of the lead roles, it was practically all I could think about.)

*She looks forward and reaches out, as if to touch someone or some-
thing she cannot see (5.128). The camera pulls slowly away. Then
her hand changes its path.*

(I made a scrapbook of pictures I had clipped from movie
magazines:)

*In extreme close-up, Marion's hand continues its movement until
it grasps the shower curtain in the left foreground of the frame
(5.129).*

(Patty reaching for a bottle of pills, tears streaming down
her face;)

*The shower curtain, unable to bear her weight, pulls away from
the supporting bar, as the hooks give way one by one (5.130).*

(Barbara Parkins in a white bathrobe, collapsed on the
beach;)

*Marion's arm falls, followed by her head and torso. Her body spills
over from within the shower, and lands on the curtain (5.131).*

(Sharon Tate in a low-cut beaded dress, her blonde hair
piled up high.)

*From (5.131), there follows a cut to the reprise of the sunburst
shot of the shower head viewed frontally.*

(Later, when the movie premiered at Grauman's Chinese, I
begged my mother to take me to see it.)

The camera cuts to Marion's legs, blood mixing with the water (5.132), and begins to move to the left, following this flow of water and blood.

("Wait till it comes to the Chatsworth Cinema," she said.)

At the moment Marion's legs are about to pass out of the frame, the drain comes into view (5.133).

(The Saturday the bodies were discovered, I saw *Arabesque*, a thriller starring Sophia Loren and Gregory Peck.)

The camera reframes to center the drain as it tracks in toward it, so that the blackness within appears about to engulf the screen (5.134).

(The "Coming Attraction" was for *Goodbye, Columbus*, a serious adult drama.)

At this point, there is a slow dissolve from the drain to an eye, viewed in extreme closeup (5.135).

(The following week, I would ride up to see it, but they wouldn't let me in. It was recommended for mature audiences.)

This eye, which fixes the camera in its gaze, displaces the drain in the frame, and appears to peer out from within it (5.136).

(We lived a few miles from the Spahn Movie Ranch.)

The camera spirals out clockwise as though unscrewing itself, disclosing the eye, Marion's, dead (5.137).

(There was a newspaper machine in front of the Chatsworth Cinema. I always chained my bicycle to it.)

The camera keeps spiraling out until we have a full view of Marion's face (5.138).

(When I left the theater that afternoon, I saw the face of Sharon Tate.)

Death has frozen it in inexpressiveness, although there is a tear welled in the corner of her eye (5.139).

(Then I read the headline as my eyes adjusted to the sun.)

7

Moonstones

for Joan Larkin

As Eileen unchains her bicycle
from the railing in front of Yaffa,
the clasp on Joan's bracelet breaks
and half a dozen moonstones
scatter at our feet.
We start to collect them, but
they're hard to see:
we keep confusing them
with tiny pieces of glass.
People pass and stare at us
as we stand there, staring
down at the sidewalk.
A drunk appears and slurs
"Whatcha lookin' for?"
"Moonstones," says Joan.
Beer in hand, he happily
joins the search.
Among the four of us,
we find five—the last one
either rolled out of sight
or (Joan begins to think)
fell off before the bracelet broke.
After about twenty minutes,
she's willing to let it go.
It's past midnight, so
she decides to take a cab

home to Brooklyn. We walk
towards 2nd Ave. At the corner,
I look back: the drunk hovers
where we left him, still trying
to locate the last moonstone
on St. Mark's Place.

Poem

I drank too much coffee
earlier in the evening
and couldn't sleep   plus
he kept tossing and turning
and saying things like "Shut up"
and "What's going on out there"
    "Damnit" I said   reaching
for a cigarette in the dark I knocked
over a glass   "Damnit"   and
all night he kept kicking me

Postcard from Cherry Grove

Ira's fed up with it here: he's already
pricing rentals for next year in The Pines.
All night, the Ice Palace's eternal disco hits
haunt our sleep—a heartbeat out of Poe, and
telltale as the three lesbians who, week before
last, broke the railing they were leaning against
and landed on the boardwalk below the club. They
were drunk and (of course) survived without a scratch.
Water taxis are still a thrill: they make me feel
like Marilyn in *Some Like It Hot*. Which
reminds me: we're having great sex, but only
after *terrible* fights. A drag queen is
screaming as I write this: "You Bitch!"

3 a.m.

Ira, this is my pillow.

Go away.

Here's yours.

Go away.

Be nice.

Why don't you roll on your side.

Because I'm just coming to bed.

Why don't you stuff a pillow in your mouth.

Be nice.

Why should I?

(I kiss his neck)

You won't remember any of this in the morning.

What Ira Said in His Sleep

1

Lights out

Brassiere too tight

2

What did you do?

What didn't you do?

Taxes

3

Indian Chief

4

Ow! Fatso!

5

Go fuck yourself!

How dare you talk to me that way!

6

Oranges

Innocuous things, mostly

7

Is it sit-down or buffet?

A Photograph

All that year
I thought I was twenty-two
till John, on one of his
visits, corrected me:
I was twenty-three.

That was also the year
I started drinking
on a daily basis.
I was still carrying on
about Tom. John
kept trying to convince me
that Tom wasn't worth it,
but it was a hopeless cause.

John also took
lots of pictures of me:
in front of my building
on O'Farrell St.,
on the Sausalito
Ferry, at Fisherman's Wharf.

He snapped this one
in a garden
in Golden Gate Park.
God, I can't believe those bangs!

Or those rose-tinted
sunglasses!
That's the denim jacket
I stole from Tops 'N Trousers
before they fired me
(I rarely showed up).

On the back
of the photograph
I wrote: *Me surrounded*
by "First Love" roses,
(our private joke)
Golden Gate Park,
San Francisco,
1976.

It

was over
yesterday

but tonight
seems all right:

     no tv

     warm sheets

     his knee in my back

     sleep-breathing

     lilacs

To order HIGH RISK Books / Serpent's Tail:
(US) 212-274-8981   (UK) 071-354-1949